# Acknowledgements

A huge thank you to the five incredible military spouses who let me pester them, ask questions and graciously provided the information for the case studies included in this book.

Thank you, from the bottom of my heart, to:

Amanda Huffman - Airman to Mom

Lizann Lightfoot - The Seasoned Spouse

Tara and Tiffany - Real Talk with the Ms's

Amy Schweizer - Tiny Troops Soccer

Kaycee McCoy - Create Captivate

For my husband, who believes in me
more than I ever could.

I love you.

# Contents

# Introduction

Life as a Military Spouse isn't always the easiest. But this book isn't about that. I didn't write it to highlight the struggles we face, because everyone faces struggles.

I didn't write it for people to feel sorry for us, or tell us "well, you knew what you were getting yourself into".

I wrote it because I believe that Military Spouses are a rare breed. I believe that everybody in this world has a purpose, a reason we are here and I believe that Military Spouses can combine that with a boat load of experiences, tribulations, adventures and projects that mean they can become the most incredible business owners and entrepreneurs.

I wrote this book to inspire you to be one of those Military Spouses and that fact that you have this book in your hands, means you believe this as well.

So, I want to help you.

I'm sure you've seen people running their successful businesses and dreamed of being where they are. Maybe you started once and gave up, maybe you're too scared to start because you don't think you'll ever make it that far. Maybe you're comparing yourself to others far too much.

Because guess what? Those successful business owners didn't just appear where they are today. They started exactly where you are now.

Throughout this book I will be sharing case studies of a number of different Military Spouses who have started their own businesses, sharing some key learnings from each one and summarising the best takeaways that you can consider when starting your own business.

I'll also share with you some important next steps that you can take, on your journey to entrepreneurship.

I will caveat this though: what works for one person won't necessarily work for another.

We are all different people, we operate differently, we have different ideas of how things should look and work. But these people are successful for a reason, so there is always something that can be learned, adapted and implemented.

This book covers Military Spouses who have:

- Started their own podcasts

- Written books and guides sharing their own experiences, to help other military spouses

- Started a soccer school for military kids

- Started their own creative design agency

This list is not exhaustive of the business possibilities, you have to listen to what it is that YOU feel drawn to do - and I'll go into this later in the book.

As you go through this book, take notes when something stands out so you can refer back to it.

I also find that I learn more from things when I read or listen to them more than once.

It's not a ridiculously long book for that reason! I want you to continue to refer back to this for more inspiration, ideas and motivation.

# Chapter 1 - A little about me.....

My goal is for this to be the shortest chapter in the book! This is not me trying to promote myself, but I feel like I may have more credibility with you if you know a bit more about my background; how and why I got to where I am.

Plus, it's always nice to know who you're actually listening to, don't you think?

I have always been Miss Independent! From the age of about 7 when I asked my parents to let me go to boarding school once my brother had gone!

I was a military brat growing up, so new homes, new countries and new friends were nothing new to me from day one!

I was always outgoing, gregarious and confident. I, also, always had to be doing something! My dad actually refers to me as a human doing rather than a human being!

I bounced off to boarding school aged eight in the end; 8 going on 21! I was at boarding school up until 18, when I then went to university, getting my first "proper" job during my placement year.

I've always wanted to work, taking on jobs where I could as soon as I was legally allowed to work. Straight out of uni I went corporate, working in Project Management and Business Development in start-ups, which took me out to Abu Dhabi in the UAE.

If you know about the UAE, I don't need to tell you! But if you don't know, it's essentially a massive adult's playground!

I spent 5 years there and my career went from strength to strength. I was working on one of Abu Dhabi's biggest projects, making a name for myself and had my sights set on CEO in the future.

My career was, and still is, a massive part of my identity and who I am.

One crazy night, after finishing a charity run with a friend, I was out at an Irish bar celebrating, as you do! Long story short, I end up meeting a man. Not just any man. The man, my man.

We met that one time, the connection was there - we both felt it - but the next day he was on a plane back to the USA.

Then begins our modern day love story of WhatsApps, Skype conversations and finally, a trip to the states for me over Christmas to actually spend some time together.

Am I crazy for travelling half way round the world to meet some stranger I met in a bar one time?

Possibly. But, when you know, you know!

I'm a firm believer in doing the things that most people would only say "what if" about.

So after a whirlwind week of first dates, it's time for me to return to the UAE, but we know there is a big decision to be made.

You see, if we want this to work in the long-term, one of us needs to leave where we are to be with the other.

What I haven't told you yet, is that this guy is in the military. So - he's not going to be leaving anywhere on his own accord at this point!

So, I make the decision to follow my heart, quit my job and leave behind my career in Abu Dhabi to make a life with this guy.

Three years later (at the time of writing) and we're happily married. But it's not been without it's struggles! Like I said earlier, my career is part of what makes me who I am. And when I came to the states, first as a tourist and then as a spouse, I was unable to work for the longest time, legally.

And that was a punch in the gut! I thought at first, I'd be OK with it, you know, an extended holiday - how awesome is that?!

Turns out, not very!

I love to work! I love to get up every day with a purpose, with a career to grow and with a sense of success each and every day. I lost this when I couldn't work. I lost myself, my feelings of worthiness and it was replace with a low self-esteem and pretty crappy attitude if I'm honest.

Add on to this, that the military literally refer to me (and all spouses) as "dependents". So I've gone from being Miss Independent, to the ultimate "dependent" and it really started to break me down!

Anyway, pity party over - I found a pretty decent job and after 3 months we had to leave because we were PCSing (moving to another military installation).

I'm sure you all know how the rest of the story goes: move to remote place with no job prospects, take jobs for minimum wage even though you're far too qualified, get frustrated, quit job, look for next, move again etc. etc.

For me, entrepreneurship was the only way that I saw that I was able to make an impact, get the professional fulfilment I so desperately craved and create something that would not only fit around this military lifestyle - but would enhance it. Would allow me to be where I needed to be, when I needed to be there; would allow me to hold down the fort back home when my husband has to up and leave to do his duty.

So I started my own business. I created an online course to help my fellow military spouses create, launch and scale their own businesses. Interestingly, while the course drew plenty of attention and created a number of success stories, the demand for my services started to focus more on help and guidance for people to create their own courses! So, my business took a natural change in direction to what it is today: I am an online course creator and 1-1 business coach, focussing on mission driven entrepreneurs and providing them with business growth and mindset development strategies.

Those of you who know me well, will know that this journey involved a lot of learning, some mistakes and a lot of tough love to realise where my skills and abilities could best serve the people that need it.

However, underlying that I have also felt a strong desire to empower and support my fellow military spouses who want to do the same thing, to start their own businesses.

So that's why I decided to write this book. To inspire you, dear reader, to look deeper into yourself, to believe in yourself, and to really understand what it is that makes you unique and what you have to offer the world, so that you can create your own successful business that beautifully compliments your crazy-amazing military adventure.

# Chapter 2 - Case Study 1 - Airman-to- Mom

In 2013, Amanda Huffman hung up her combat boots and traded them for nappy bags and changing tables. After 6 years of serving in the US Air Force, as a dual-military couple, Amanda made the decision to stay at home and raise her family as her husband continued to serve.

I can believe Amanda when she says that she thought it would be a welcome change, but soon after leaving she lost part of her identity. Leaving any job is hard; leaving the military which is a lifestyle, intense and where Amanda was an officer, to a whole new way of life, must have been a huge shock to the system.

Amanda has a degree in Civil Engineering and deployed to Afghanistan to help rebuild the war-torn nation.

Can you imagine going from rebuilding cities in the Middle East to changing nappies in the middle of the night? I mean no disrespect to stay-at-homes mums, I truly believe they have one of the hardest jobs in the world. I mean the change of pace, the change of demands, the change of role.

Amanda says in her own words: "When I left the Air Force after 6 years of service my plan was to be a military spouse and stay at home mom. But when I left the military, I lost a part of my identity and started to rediscover myself through writing".

This is where her journey into entrepreneurship begins. After just a few months of being out of the Air Force and a full time MilSpouse and SAHM, she was ready for her next challenge. At first it started with just 5 minutes of writing a week. She was part of an online forum, and through her writing and engagement, she began making connections with other women and began to learn more about starting her own business.

It is these connections that contributed to the longevity of her business. Amanda admits that she thought having a business would be an "easy" way to bring in money and support the family - an assumption many of us make. The reality was much more difficult, but she stayed doing what she was doing because of the connections she had made.

What's also interesting is that although Amanda is a solo entrepreneur (she is the only one involved in her business) she soon realised that trying to build a business entirely on your own is far from easy, and one of the loneliest things you can do. She soon realised that it's not fun on your own, you have no support group and nobody to bounce ideas off.

We should also be incredibly grateful for the support group that Amanda found, as she says that if it wasn't for this group of people she's met along the way, she would have quit a long time ago - imagine the lives that she wouldn't have impacted.

Because that is what is at the heart of what Amanda does - she tells other people's stories, to share their impact and inspire others. Since Amanda left the military, she found that her calling is to share the stories of others; other women specifically, who have served in the military.

Her podcast "Women in the Military" is a compilation of over 50 different stories, from different women, who have had different experiences in the military, both good and bad. Some of these stories are hard to tell, because they are painful; but Amanda's reason for doing this is to help answer the questions that some people are too afraid, or don't even know to ask - when they are thinking about joining the military, or just want to know what life in this crazy world is like!

On top of this Amanda has created a number of free resources around deployments, PCSing, life after the military, and a girls guide to joining the military - just to help and reach more people.

Her business was born out of a desire to help people that she knew needed help, and that she was able to help - this is a massive ingredient in the recipe for success!

When I asked Amanda why she chose entrepreneurship over a career, her response is both beautiful and not uncommon among military spouses: "My degree is in Civil Engineering and I could have probably found a good 9 to 5 job, but I wanted to be home with my kids. I like the flexibility of entrepreneurship where I can set my schedule and be there for my kids the way I want to be. We planned for me to not work so having that foundation made entrepreneurship an adventure and not something that I had to make succeed. For me being an entrepreneur is following my passion and making an impact. I didn't think I could find that working in a typical office. And it has worked great for me and our family."

My favourite word here is "flexibility" - entrepreneurship isn't easy, and anyone who tells you otherwise is lying. Amanda is not saying that she chose it because it was easier then having a job; but that it afforded her the flexibility to be at home with her children, whilst creating her own success and following her dreams.

So after a career in the military, becoming a stay-at-home mum, starting a podcast, writing a book, inspiring so many people, I'm sure you're wondering what Amanda's biggest achievement has been.

Here's what she said: "I thought that serving in the military and deploying to Afghanistan would be the capstone of my life and never realized it was just the beginning. I think going through the fear and launching my podcast even though I was worried it would be a failure and no one would listen was a big achievement. I never dreamed it would hit 12,000 downloads within the first year and that it would open doors to so many different opportunities."

How many people can say that a deployment to Afghanistan was just the start of the greatest things you'll go on to achieve.

When you look at it like that, entrepreneurship as a military spouse seems pretty freaking exciting doesn't it??

I asked Amanda what the best piece of advice she'd ever received was, so we could share it with you.

"When you come to a great chasm in life, jump, it really isn't that far".

This served her both when she was in Afghanistan and ever since and I think it's great. Fear holds so many of us back from great things, but we really shouldn't be afraid - the thing on other side isn't really that scary, and you'll never get to know if you don't just go for it!

<u>So what can we learn from Amanda?</u>

1.  A business idea can be built from passion. If you have a real desire to serve a community, to help, to inspire - in a completely selfless way, then it is possible for something incredibly real and impactful to be created.

2.  Being a solo entrepreneur isn't easy. If this is the way your business is structured, or starts out, try and find a support network - either online or in person - to bounce ideas off, hold yourself accountable and talk you out of the those places that you will inevitably tiptoe towards, regularly.

3.  Entrepreneurship means exploring multiple different business streams. Amanda doesn't only have the podcast, she has also written a book, hosts a blog on her website and offers numerous free resources for her community.

4.  Carrying on from 3 - not everything in your business is about making money. Free resources should be part and parcel of any business; giving to your community in exchange for nothing. Businesses born out of a genuine purpose and passion to help people, have far more longevity and provide much

more satisfaction for the person running it!

# Chapter 3 - Case Study 2 - Seasoned Spouse

For those of you who have been around the military for a while, this next entrepreneur will need no introduction! For those of you who are newer to this, let me present Lizann Lightfoot, aka, The Seasoned Spouse.

Lizann began The Seasoned Spouse blog in 2016, during her husband's 6th deployment; her family (which included at the time: her, her husband and four children) had just returned to the states after being overseas for 3 years.

No stranger to the military lifestyle, Lizann and her husband met in 2000, married in 2007 so when she started the blog, she had 15 years experience as a military spouse - I think you'll agree that "Seasoned Spouse" is a very appropriate name.

Initially, she wanted to provide a checklist of things for spouses to consider, to help them adjust to the new unit. A lot of the newer spouses were coming to her with questions and concerns about their first deployments. So she decided to tailor the blog to supporting military loved ones, while also providing a professional platform and a potential source of income for her family.

Just 3 months after starting her blog she had an offer for her first freelance article and within 9 months, she had an offer for a part-time writing job! Talk about rapid growth!

Lizann didn't just wake up one day and decide she wanted to write for a living. It was always something she had been interested in and was good at. She self-published a book in 2014 and had plans for many more. This point is worth noting if you're thinking of going down the blogging route - do you enjoy writing and are you good at it? (That means, does someone you don't know, enjoy your writing?)

When I say enjoy, I don't mean do you enjoy the romantic idea of being snuggled up by a fire, wrapped in a blanket drinking wine as you pen your novel; I mean does the idea of creating new content excite you? Do you have words and ideas rolling around in your head all day? Are you prepared to deal with writer's block?

Blogging isn't easy. It's not just a question of writing an article and waiting for people to come and read it. There's marketing, SEO (Search Engine Optimisation - how well your site performs in a search engine), website design and development and much more. I'm not saying this to put you off, I believe blogging is an amazing outlet to share your story and to inspire others, I just don't want you to think it will be a walk in the park.

For Lizann, writing wasn't the hard part; that came second nature to her.

For Lizann, it was the technical side of things. She had to learn from scratch how to start, develop and run a website, as the business wasn't making money at first she couldn't afford to pay anyone, so YouTube and Google became her best friends! (You won't believe how many times I've heard seasoned entrepreneurs say this!).

The other major learning curve? Collaboration among the military community. I have to say through my own experience as well, that no matter what it is you do for your business, everybody in this community wants to see you succeed! Podcasters supporting other podcasters, bloggers writing for each other, writers all pushing one another to the next big thing.

Lizann said it perfectly: "when we work together, we all succeed". And it's so true. So if you're struggling right now and you're trying to go it alone, reach out to your local military community, or find a great online one - there's an abundance of people just waiting to help you!

And Lizann will tell you that writing is an amazing opportunity for military spouses. She chose the entrepreneurial route over the traditional career path because of her babies. She had 4 when she started writing, she now has 5! Writing allowed her to stay home, to tap into her creativity, to look after her babies and make some money while her husband was away - all while helping people through her writing.

When her business began and the children were small she would write whenever and wherever she could - evenings, nap times, around school pick ups and eventually picked up a steady stream of clients.

When you want something badly enough - you'll find a way to make it happen, no excuses.

Throughout The Seasoned Spouse's career, there have been many, many accomplishments. The most notable for Lizann is finishing her book "Open When…..you love someone in the military". It is her first traditionally published book and has been a labour of love, spanning 2 years of writing, a deployment, a PCS and the birth of her fifth baby. You just know it's going to be a good one!

This is also a prime example that no matter what the military throws in your path, all you need to do is adapt and overcome, to make sure you can still achieve your goals.

So, what advice does Lizann have for you if you're thinking of starting your own blog?

'You can do it.' Sometimes, you just need someone to believe in your goal and take you seriously. Of course my husband has always been my biggest supporter. But when I was just getting started I met another milspouse who had recently published a book. She had run a website for years and was a role model to me. After looking at my blog and hearing about my project ideas, she told me, "You can definitely write a book, and I would be very interested to read it!" Hearing those words from another successful writer helped make my dream feel possible. It took a while, but a few years later I did finish my book and it got picked up by a publisher!"

YOU CAN DO IT. It really is that simple. Now go out and prove it for yourself.

<u>What can we learn from Lizann?</u>

1. Being a mother should, in no way, hold you back from starting and growing your own business. Find time in your day to create your dream, and don't stop until you've made it!

2. Find a community - within the military or outside. People who will support your goals, and whose goals you can support too. Share ideas, resources and platforms to grow your presence.

3.  "You can do it"! Find someone who supports you and your goals no matter how crazy they may seem. Sometimes starting a business can really get us down and carrying on seems impossible. Have that person in your corner who will keep pushing you on and believing in you. No matter what.

# Chapter 4 - Case Study 3 - Real Talk with the Ms's

The second podcast that I wanted to highlight, for a number of reasons, is called Real Talk with the Ms's, because that's exactly what it is!

You are about to see how:

1 - This one demonstrates the beauty and benefits of a 2-woman show when it comes to running a business

2 - You don't have to live in the same state to make it work

3 - To keep things REAL!

4 - Podcasts are such an incredible opportunity.

One of the newest businesses in the bunch, but no less impressive let me tell you!

In April of 2019 Tiffany called Tara, just like she always did. These two have been friends for a long time and when military life separated them, they continued their "long-distance relationship" over FaceTime, phone calls etc.

It was during one of these calls that Tiffany bought up the idea of a podcast. Tiff had recently moved to a new location with her husband and didn't find that sense of community. We've all been there, some places seem to do it really well and in others, the sense of community just doesn't exist; it's lonely.

She hadn't gone back to work yet and had been listening to a lot of different podcasts in her free time and the realisation hit her, that there was nothing for her to listen to. Nothing that really spoke to her and resonated with what she was going through. So, in the spirit of any driven entrepreneur, she suggested they do it themselves!

She asked Tara if she was interested, and pitched it as "we'll just have our same conversations and just record them and share them with the community". What I love is that these two had no idea where it would go, if anywhere, but they saw a need and they wanted to fill the gap - if you've heard their podcast you'll be grateful they did, and if you haven't, well you need to!

When we listen to podcasts, we don't realise the work that goes into them! It's more than just recording a conversation - there's editing, planning, cutting, merging, marketing and so much more. Tara and Tiffany realised this shortly after starting but it didn't stop them.

Tiffany works as a nurse and Tara looks after the children and holds down the fort at home; neither of these things leave much time for extra-activities but they both love and believed in this idea so much that they found a way to make it work.

THAT's part of the key to success. Many of us start businesses while we're still working because we can't afford to make the leap; and it's hard! Working, raising a family, being a wife - all of these things take work and dedication, so add one more thing into the mix and it starts to rack up!

But these two power-women pressed on because they KNEW there was gap they wanted to fill and they were determined to make it happen

See that? Hard work and determination. No magic pill, no secret blueprint for success. Good, old fashioned hard work.

One of the things they had to work through, one of their biggest learnings was creating their personal and professional boundaries. Learning how to be business partners with your best friend, telling them things in a work capacity that you don't want them to take personally. Something that they will both openly tell you that they struggled with.

So they found a solution! The found an app called Marco Polo, which allowed them to communicate with each other using voice notes, so messages weren't misinterpreted as you can hear the tone in the other person's voice. I think this is such a smart move, and potentially something that strengthened their relationship in the long run.

The other thing to consider in a partner is your respective role in the partnership. At first, Tiffany and Tara struggled with this and what their combined overall vision for the podcast was. The realised that the vision can change and evolve and grow - and that's OK.

My friend, I can't stress this enough! Your business will most likely look a lot different in 2 years than it does now, and that's absolutely OK!

Of course you know, this book is about entrepreneurship as a military spouse and I'm so intrigued to know what makes people choose the path of starting their own business.

For Tara, as soon as she had her babies she struggled getting up and leaving them every day, something many of us can relate to! Add into the mix the challenge of being married to someone in the military and you're faced with the potential of your children growing up with both parents gone from the home each day - this was something that Tara didn't want to have to do. For her, she wanted to find a way to contribute to the family that she loves, and do it around their schedules in a way that works for everyone.

For Tiff, it was about making a difference in the lives of people who she felt were experiencing the same struggles that she had, that had no outlet or source of support. Military life can be hard sometimes - something most of you are painfully aware of I'm sure - and often the struggle can be exacerbated when we don't find our people, or someone who understands where we're coming from or what we're going through. Tiff wanted to change that. She wanted to share herself, her relationship with Tara and their everyday struggles, in the hope of touching the lives of others and speaking to those who really need it.

It's still early days for these two, just over a year in business, but they are making a real impact. They are talking about things that people in this community want and need to hear and I'm pleased to say they aren't slowing down anytime soon!

So, if you're thinking about starting your own podcast - military related or not, here's what The Real Talk with The Ms's want you to know: bring IN resources to your podcast, find other people to interview and expand your network that way.

If you're looking for examples of how they did this; one of their biggest and favourite interviews was with Dr. Chapman author of "5 Love Languages". They spoke to him about his military specific version of this book - so you can imagine how well received that was among the military community. Exactly the type of people

Tara and Tiffany want to help, in exactly the way they set out to help them.

<u>What can we learn from Real Talk with The Ms's?</u>

1.  If you want to do something badly enough, just start and figure out how to do it! These ladies admit that the struggled with some of technical aspects of the podcast, but they didn't let this hold them back. They persevered, they learned and they pressed on.You can do the same! There are so

many resources out there, so many people who want to see you succeed - find what works for you and just go for it!

2.  If you're looking for something you need and you can't find it anywhere - go and create it yourself. Chances are if you want it, others do too. Find the gap, then find out how to fill it.

3.  Partnerships are incredible for businesses, but they take work. If you're going into business with your best friend, be open, honest and respectful to your partner and

create clear and agreed boundaries from the start.

# Chapter 5 - Case Study 4 - Tiny Troops Soccer

Our next, and perhaps most far-reaching in terms of the locations covered, case study is Amy Schweizer, Founder and CEO of Tiny Troops

Soccer (TTS). Some of you parents may have already crossed paths with Amy's organisation, due to its vast network across the military community.

TTS is a developmental soccer program that focuses on not only teaching children the basic skills of soccer, but also develops their spatial awareness, gross motor skills and social interaction skills; the goal is not only sports, but teaching children from an early age how to integrate with others - to thrive in social situations.

Although Amy is a military spouse, and TTS schools are located around military installations, the classes are open to everyone! Classes are offered on specific bases for people with military IDs, as well as off-base for the civilian population.

 Amy's "why" behind starting her business will resonate with many of you, it certainly does with me! She was a consummate career woman before she married into the military and for some (not all, I appreciate this) but for many, the two really don't coincide. Constant PCS moves, frequent times of solo parenting and even the mere mention of the term "military spouse" during an interview can spell the end before it's even started

It was when Amy was at her second duty station, pregnant with their second child and 5 years into military spouse life that she decided she needed some form of job because she just didn't feel fulfilled.

Raise your hand if you've felt like this at any point!

She was presented with the opportunity to coach children's soccer and after some time, she realised that she could turn this into a full blown career; a business in fact. Amy has always been sporty, and finding a place to direct her passions and her energy really started to fill that gap that a lack of career had created.

Amy's ultimate career dream was to work in the Community Relations Department of a professional sports team. She has a Master's Degree in Sport Management and, unfortunately for Amy, in order to pursue a career in this field one needs to be located in or near a major city.

As most of you will know, the majority of military installations are not located in areas that are in or near the sorts of places that Amy would need to be to make this career her reality. And if she was, chances are it would be short-lived with the next PCS.

So, through the initially lack of choice regarding her dream career combined with the opportunity to coach soccer to children and a real drive and passion to make a difference and achieve the life she wanted; in 2015 Tiny Troops Soccer was born!

Now, starting TTS was not without its challenges. Starting any business is hard, but throw in trying to start a business and operating out of certain military installations, working with children and training new soccer coaches….well, there was a lot to deal with.

But Amy didn't see this as a reason to give up. She decided that in no uncertain terms she would not take "no" for an answer. She was creating something to benefit the children and families of the military and surrounding communities and she was going to do whatever it took to make it happen!

It's an unfortunate reality, but there is still a vast proportion of the military and its affiliates that is used to the more traditional spouse roles. This is absolutely NOT something that I have an issue with. However, there are spouses who are creating their own careers through entrepreneurship and whilst this is becoming more accepted, it can often slow things down for people trying to work with the military and grow their businesses through the installations.

What does this mean? Paperwork. Lots and lots and lots of paperwork.

But as Amy has shown us; you don't have to take no for an answer. Push back, ask the questions and eventually you may get the answer you want. Albeit under a mountain of paperwork - but that's totally worth it.

I asked Amy what's one piece of advice that she's received, that she wants to share with you in your journey of starting your own business. Sit down for this because it's so good!

"Do the NEXT right thing. We're all going to make mistakes and bad choices. You can either choose to stay and wallow in that, or move forward doing the best you can."

Absolutely brilliant! I talk about failure a lot and how it's necessary in order to move forward, but this piece of advice adds another layer and makes it so explicit that bad mistakes/choices/decisions are inevitable. It's how we deal with and move on from them that determines our success.

How successful? Well in the 5 years that Tiny Troops Soccer has been in business, it is currently employing over 100 military spouses! The military community is at the heart of this organisation and I truly believe it's only just getting started.

<u>What can we learn from Tiny Troops Soccer?</u>

1.  Starting a business that requires affiliation with/agreement from/ working with the military is full of

challenges. But don't let this be a reason to hold you back. Stay focused on the overall goal of the organisation, keep asking questions in different ways and to different people and find the light at the end of the tunnel.

2. Entrepreneurship among military spouses is on the rise, hugely, and now is the perfect time to be a part of this amazing movement - so don't let anything else hold you back.

3. Think about your business in terms of the impact it can have on your peers and community. TTS is not

only teaching the community's little ones how to play soccer; it's providing employment opportunities for the people that Amy cares deeply about. Focus on giving back.

# Chapter 6 - Case Study 5 - Create Captivate

Our last, but by no means least, milspouse is the absolute go-getter: Kaycee McCoy, founder and CEO of Create Captivate, a digital marketing agency. Create Captivate is your "one stop shop for the digital marketing needs of any small business".

Kaycee's story is slightly different from our other military spouses in that she was a business owner before she was a military spouse, however, that doesn't make her story any less inspirational. In fact, I believe Kaycee had to overcome a wide range of different obstacles in order to maintain the crazy entrepreneur lifestyle that she was so ingrained in, whilst getting the hand of the whole military "thing".

Kaycee's entrepreneurial journey started back when she was just 9 years old; she began Kards by Kaycee when her parents purchased a new design software and she started designing cards, flyers and calendars. Unfortunately, that childlike bravado and massive confidence got a little lost as Kaycee grew up - haven't we all been there?

When Kaycee was in her mid-twenties, her and her (now) husband were moved to Virginia Beach, thanks to the Navy, and Kaycee relied of staffing agencies to find work. She was offered a role as soon as they arrived in VB so she jumped at the chance. The idea of having a job surpassed the importance of how that job aligned with her long-term career goals or, in fact, it didn't. How many of you milspouses out there can relate to that? I know I absolutely can.

It was during one of these jobs that Kaycee got the swift kick up the backside that she didn't realise she needed until after the fact. Whilst working for a janitorial company, she wasn't surprised to note that her creative juices were not rumbled when talking about toilet paper! As good as she was at her job, she always felt called to do more, to offer more. She wanted to create flyers for the company, edit or update their website, make promo videos for YouTube - quick tip: if you can't get an idea out of your head, chances are it's something you should be pursuing for yourself!

Anyway, back to Kaycee….! She ended up creating a few things for the company, using her initiative, not because she was asked, and was sharing these with one of her companies sales reps. In turn, he pointed out how great her work was and suggested she could help out a few of his friends who have businesses. Kaycee jumped at the opportunity and created a CD ROM (remember those?!) of her work.

Once her colleague had shown this to his contact, he reached out to Kaycee to arrange a meeting and shortly after they started working together - her first official client and the start of her own journey into entrepreneurship.

It wasn't an easy start though. Kaycee was burning the candle at every end, holding onto her day job as well as working with that first client. The problem was not her skill set or abilities AT ALL....it was her mindset. She kept herself small, telling herself that it was all she could handle and it was better to play it safe.

In 2017 though she decided enough was enough and it was time to step into her own greatness. She re-branded, leased an office space and started building her business into the successful Create Captivate we see today: award-winning agency, with a small team of employees and freelancers who serve clients all over the globe.

So what was it that helped Kaycee from where she was discussing toilet paper and creating designs on the side, to running her own successful agency? The answer shouldn't surprise you. SUPPORT.

Entrepreneurship can be such a lonely way of life, working from home (often) and not engaging with others can be extremely detrimental. Networking is unbelievably necessary!

Kaycee became a member of the Milspo Project in Hampton Roads and describes it as a "breath of fresh air". It was a network of like-minded people to set goals with, attend events together and experience all the ups and downs of entrepreneurship. On top of this, Kaycee sought out mentors, a therapist and a Life Coach. Through all of these amazing experiences, Kaycee has not only found her place, but that of her business as well and truly feels like a part of her community.

It's this that makes a business beautiful. It's not just the service you provide, but the way that your business becomes such an integral part of your life and adds an extra layer of fulfilment to you as you immerse yourself in communities and activities that you would never have previously considered.

What was it that made Kaycee go full force into entrepreneurship? She has plenty of jobs and was highly employable, so why not take the "less risky" route and seek employment? Interestingly, Kaycee feels that it was actually entrepreneurship that chose her! She was surrounded by it growing up with both parents being business-owners, so she never really understood that scary aspect of owning your now business, it was something people did.

It wasn't fear of failure  that held her back for the longest time, but fear of success. I think this is something that affects a lot of us, sometimes without even realising that's what it is. When you really think about it, success is actually scarier isn't it? If you fail, you have an excuse to give up and go back to comfortable. If you're successful, well you just have to keep going!

For Kaycee, it was frustration with toxic work environments and the lack of autonomy that being an employee brought, that was the driving force behind her going it alone. She thrives on the ability to change "how things have always been done", to solve problems the way she sees fit and be able to evolve, adapt and create.

Entrepreneurship for Kaycee provided the ability to continue to learn, to feed her curiosity and to ultimately be responsible for every decision - good or bad. For some people, that sounds terrible, but I just know that the entrepreneurs reading this are vigorously nodding their heads giving me all the "mmhmmmms"!

And for the days you feel like giving up? Read this, again and again: "the idea that I could steer the ship and curate a company culture of my own was the biggest driving factor for me at the time and is still the biggest motivation for me on the rare days when I feel like giving up."

The most wonderful thing I learned about Kaycee throughout this, is this: Her favourite part of entrepreneurship, the thing she considers to be her biggest achievement is not her biggest contract, it's not her first client or a huge paycheck. It's hiring her first employee in 2018. It's being able to contribute to someone else's livelihood. How incredibly selfless and gracious is that?

To leave you with Kaycee's best piece of advice, I feel really needs to be done in her own words. Essentially, don't over complicate and over think things to the point you have talked ourself out of it.

She paints a far better picture: "One of my very best friends sat down with me during the early fall of 2015 when I was enduring the absolute most soul-sucking burnout and frustration I have still ever felt as an entrepreneur.  She is the polar opposite of me in so many ways and I think that is what makes our friendship so magical.  Her logical, super no nonsense way of thinking is such a beautiful contrast to my ideas-galore, pie-in-the-sky personality.

She's my go-to when I'm feeling like my head is going to pop straight off my shoulders and roll down the street with sheer anxiety or too many to do's.  On that fall afternoon as we kicked back on my living room sofa and started to kick around business talk, she helped me have one of the most life-altering epiphanies I have ever experienced in business.

At the time I was drowning in my own head.  Business was scarce to say the least and the work I did have was frustrating at best.  Tears were flowing down my face as I shared my inner dreams + hopes of what my business could be someday, but didn't even remotely resemble at the time.  She asked me what of ALL the things I wanted to do and change would make the biggest, best impact up front and help shift everything else.  My answer was workshops.  Along with entrepreneurship, teaching seems to be a genetic trait for me.  I had always dreamed of teaching workshops and helping small business owners learn to navigate the dizzying world of social media and marketing.  However, the big picture of such an undertaking had me thoroughly intimidated.  That's where my friend's sage advice came into play.  When she prompted me with the simple question of, "What do you need to make a workshop happen?"  I quickly replied, "A day.  A time.  A location.  A presentation."

FOUR THINGS.  Only 4 things had held me back for years!  A total palm to forehead moment, my friend bluntly asked me if I realized how wildly possible it was to tackle those four checkboxes on my to do list.  Lucky for me, the first location I asked was 100% for it and my first workshop was launched about 1.5 months later!"

<u>What can we learn from Kaycee?</u>

1.  Get out of your own head sometimes, talk it out, you have no idea when the answer will come and smack you in the face!

2.  Network, network, network! Get out of the house, or wherever you're working and meet people.

3.  We can be our own worst enemies sometimes and will often talk ourselves out of our own success. If you can recognise this and manage your own Imposter Syndrome, you will see yourself achieve things that you never

thought you'd achieve (or that you

wouldn't let yourself see!)

# Chapter 7 - What can we learn from the case studies?

The goal of this book is twofold:

1 - To show you that entrepreneurship is a very real possibility as a military spouse and to inspire YOU, dear

reader, to find your purpose and create your own entrepreneurial journey.

2 - To help give you the tools you'll need to get started.

So; what can we learn from the 5 incredible businesses covered in this book?

## Do it because you love it

Whilst all the businesses discussed in the case studies are successful, not one of them stated that the reason for starting their businesses was to make money.

It is my opinion that if you start a business with the sole purpose and intention of making money, it's a high-speed ticket to failure. Why? Because if you're chasing money then you're not in love with the process. You're not obsessed with your clients and giving them the best service possible, you're focussed on getting paid a lot, and fast.

Desperation stinks and people can tell if you're invested in their success or you see them a walking wad of cash.

Here's the other thing; very very few business will even breakeven in their first year - let alone turn a huge profit.

If you're so busy focusing on the numbers and all you see is red, then chances are you'll quit before your business fails you.

These businesses were born out of a desire to truly help people. Whether it was people who were about to go through what they had been through; not being able to find the resources so creating them themselves; wanting to share the stories of other inspirational people; giving back to the military community through a love of sport or sharing a passion for design to help boost businesses' marketing.

This is what is at the true heart of entrepreneurship: impacting, helping and providing for others. Not the pay check.

However, what these businesses did realise is that where there is a demand for something, they should be charging their worth and rightly so.

You see, whilst the businesses began out of a desire to help others, all of them are providing a service, giving their time and impacting the lives of others. When you provide value to people, when you give your time, knowledge and experience that you have worked hard for, when your pour yourself into something, you deserve to be compensated for this.

But, the exchange is based on the giving of value NOT on the price tag that you're chasing.

Do something because you love it and because it's the right thing to do. Don't do it because you need to get paid.

It's not easy flying solo

I know that when I started out in my business, I took for granted how isolating it can be. When you're so obsessed with something it can be all-consuming. You're so focussed on it that you sort of "forget" about the outside world!

However, once the initial excitement wears off, you realise how lonely you are.

So a huge thing to take from everyone in this book is networking! Formal and informal - go to official networking events to meet people in the same field or situation as you (at the time of writing we are in the midst of Coronavirus, so hopefully by now these events are a thing again!)

Create your own get togethers where you live locally; arrange coffee mornings to talk about what's going on in your businesses at the time.

Network online. There are so many forums and opportunities to meet and engage with people from your own home as well. Just don't solely rely on these, there's something very special about human interaction that the online world just can't recreate.

Search Facebook and LinkedIn for an idea of local events or networking groups and just start showing up!

These are the networks, the communities that you can turn to when you need help - and believe me there will be plenty of times you need help!

Remember Amanda (Airman to Mom) explaining that if it wasn't for one of these networking groups, she may have given up on her whole business?

These groups are here for support and also for an entrepreneur's mental health. All solopreneurs understand the challenges of working on your own, day in day out. These groups are not just to talk business, but to give you an outlet to engage with other people! As business owners we don't get the usual "office banter" (unless you have a particularly entertaining dog or child!), no water coolers chats and no 5 minute catch ups as you walk past a colleagues desk. By finding your network of people, you can create your own version of this and let me tell you it is a beautiful, beautiful thing.

## Ask for help

Please don't be too proud to ask someone for help! When you become a business-owner, some people have this sense of "well now I need to know everything" and by asking questions, it suggests they don't have it all figured out.

(I know this because it was me at first!)

Look at the case studies too - how many of them Googled, YouTubed and asked ALL the questions when they started out? Asking questions doesn't mean you don't know, it means you want to know as much as possible.

In this day and age there are SO MANY resources for people starting out in business, from the Government run Small Business Association, to mentorship programs, to smaller more intimate groups, to business coaches. There is literally something for everyone - some of it's free and some of it you pay for.

One thing I will advise is that if you go down the Business Coach route: do your research! There are some incredible coaches out there, people who genuinely care about your success and providing with the best support, tools and resources that you need.

There are also some absolute snakes who just want your money.

So research, ask, snoop and do some more research, get on the phone with them, interview them and make them work for you, before you've even hired them!

Regardless of how you get your help, just get some! Don't think that you know it all - even if you know a massive amount, you can always always learn more. And the more you learn, the better the experience that you pass on to your clients and, after all, that's what this is all about.

<u>How can your experiences help others?</u>

The thing that will make your business unique is you. You and your experiences.

Take another look at each case study. Are they the only people in the world offering these services? No. BUT they are the only ones offering their services in the way that they do.

Each business we've covered has built upon their own experiences, their skills and knowledge, their needs and their struggles and has created their very own unique and standout business as a result.

So, if you're holding back from starting a business because there are already plenty of people doing what you want to do you need to realise something. Do you know what it is that these business don't have?

YOU!

Everything that has happened to you in life up until this point is what will shape, mould and make your business stand out.

So think:

- What have you been through in life that can add to your story, that you can use to help others?

- What makes you different from everybody out there?

- What was something that you struggled with, or without - can you help others through the same situation? Can you provide them with the thing they need?

- What are you good at? What comes naturally to you and how can you harness that to share with, or teach to others?

- What gap have you identified that you're qualified to fill? Note that when I say qualified here, I don't mean that you've got the degree or the certification; I mean that you have been through the same or similar experiences and can support, teach, guide others based on what you learned in your journey.

To follow on from the last bullet point, look at what formal qualifications you could achieve to support your own experiences. For example, if you're thinking of Life Coaching, maybe consider an NLP qualification in order

to find the best ways to
communication with different clients.

Take me for example, I have 15 years
Project Management experience and a
Masters degree, but I recently
completed my PMP certification -
because you can never know too
much!

So, look at what you already know or
do well, then see if there is anything
you can do to add to this - to make
you further stand out from the crowd.

Don't, however, use this as an excuse
to hold you back! "Oh I'll start when
I've got this qualification, or I've

passed that exam". No! Start now, get the qualifications as you go and include it as part of your story - show your clients how much you care about them by going above and beyond to get EVEN MORE knowledge.

## If you want it enough, you'll find a way

You can often tell how much somebody wants something, by the sacrifices they are prepared to make.

It's all well and good paying lip service to an idea, but until your actions speak louder than your words, it's really just a lot of hot air!

You see, many people don't often give the nitty gritty details about the challenges of starting and running your own business, especially as a military spouse. Often we like to show people how "together" we have it all, swimming gracefully on top of the water as everything flails around under the surface.

In these case studies, I could be accused of glossing over many of the details that delve into the specific details of how each business started. I don't believe that is my story to tell.

But I will tell you from my own experience that there are times where it is one of the hardest things you'll ever do. In the last year my business has changed completely; it took some hard lessons, a few ego checks and an ongoing battle against throwing in the towel.

Maybe you'll have an amazing idea, but the people you've created it for don't see it the same way; maybe you won't know how to properly share your idea with the world, so nobody really understands what it is you are offering; maybe you'll get turned down for your first funding request and think that signals the end of the road for you.

This is when you have to really evaluate how much you REALLY want this. And this will also show you how much you really want it. For me, the idea of not finding a way, not finding my purpose and not creating my business was far more painful than any failures.

I wanted and I needed this, not just for me, but for the people that I knew I could help, support and impact along the way. It always comes back to my "why".

Your "why" is the foundation and the ultimate reason for creating your business. It could be a group of people you feel called to serve, it could be an experience you went through that you feel called to support others through, it could be making family members proud, or it could be the knowledge that when your spouse is deployed, they have the peace of mind that everything at home is under control.

Whatever it is, your "why" needs to be rock solid and it has to be revisited every single time you consider giving up. Because there will be times, lots of them I'm afraid. Your "why" will be what makes or breaks you. Every single time.

<u>Businesses can (and must!) be PCS proof</u>

I have often wondered, and even asked a few military spouses why they had chosen not to start their own businesses. I don't just mean I walked up to random people on the street and accused them of not doing something - these were people who I knew wanted to start their own business, just hadn't yet.

A common theme among all of them was that they didn't know how to start-up again every time they moved, so they were going to wait until their spouse had retired and they were settled somewhere.

This honestly breaks my heart to hear this. Amazing people are putting their lives and their dreams on hold because of their circumstance, but it doesn't have to be this way!

In this day and age there are so many resources available to help you either:

- Create an online business

- Provide support to you as you are in the process of moving your business

- Guide you as you re-establish yourself in a new area

- Foster genuine working and professional relationships with people all over the world

- Manage process for people, regardless of their location

- Provide services for people in multiple different time zones

- Communicate with people all over the globe

- Get reimbursed some certain licensing fees

- Operate in a state different to the
  one you formed in

And so much more!

Don't let the military lifestyle be the reason you delay following your dreams and your purpose. Not only is this unfair for you, but also for the people who are crying out for someone like you in their life right now.

All the case studies here have not just survived, but thrived in the military lifestyle, throughout numerous PCS moves. Consider what you offer, what your strengths are, then figure out how you can offer this service online, virtually or from multiple locations as you move to each one.

Engage in your community as soon as you get to a new area, network before you move.

Every problem has a solution, and there are so many people, organisations, groups and networks willing to help you find yours.

# Chapter 8 - What do you need to know to start?

More often than not, the reason so many people take so long to start, or just never do, is because they don't know what the first thing to do is.

There really isn't one specific thing that you need to do in order to start, which I know isn't particularly helpful. But there are some things that you'll want to consider before you get started, please note the following is not an exhaustive list, just something to get you going!

<u>Get super clear on why you are doing this</u>

I touched on this before, but it's that important, it's worth mentioning again. Take the time now, to get really clear about your "Why". The real reason behind your business. The one thing that you know, no matter what struggles you come up against, will ensure that you push through.

For me, ultimately it's my husband. But perhaps not in the way you might think. Yes, obviously I want to make him proud but it's more than that. His job, can be incredibly dangerous at times, to the point I actually don't want to think about it. During the early stages of our relationship, when he was deployed and I was stuck in Washington unable to work, there were times where it was a real strain in our relationship. He was away from home, doing who-knows-what trying to focus on the mission and I was complaining about not being able to work, having no purpose and generally feeling pretty sorry for myself.

So, not only was my husband doing his duty in the middle of nowhere, his mind was also back home, worrying about me: my mental-health, my happiness, if I was going to stay. The guilt I feel now for making him go through that is pretty intense.

Now, I continue to push through with my business and make it a success because I feel confident that when my husband is away now, he can focus 100% on his mission because everything is taken care of back home.

I have my business and my purpose and I have an income of my own. He no longer needs to worry and can give everything he needs to his mission.

That is my "why".

Really think about what yours is, above the mission of your business. And please, if it's money, I urge you to re-think, because it is not enough to get you through that hard times!

## Clarify your mission

Spend some time really nailing down what it is that you do. What is the purpose of your business and how do you intend to do it? This should be able to be narrowed down into a very succinct mission statement - no more than a paragraph. This is your business' pledge, who you intend to help and how to intend to help them.

The reason I say to spend some time on this and not rush it, is because your mission statement will under-pin everything that you do toward your business. You want to make sure that you have it spot on from the start, in order to keep you on track and ensure you are always working toward your mission.

That's not to say that your mission may not change over time, that's OK, but from day one, you want to have it accurately mapped out, in order to guide your work.

## Research the market

Once you know exactly what it is you want to do, you need to understand if there is a real market for it. Oftentimes, what one person thinks is a great business idea, doesn't necessarily translate into a successful business idea.

The only way you can find out if your business has legs, is to ask your target audience. It really is that simple! It's also why getting your mission statement accurate from day one is so important. Once you have honed in on your target audience, you know exactly who to ask.

In this day and age, access to your market is essentially unrestricted. You can create focus groups through social media platforms or even in person. You can create polls, run interactive live events and run beta-programs to have people test your product or service for free in exchange for feedback and reviews.

You need to ensure that you get feedback from a significant sample size in order to know if the results carry any weight. That means that you need to include a few more people than just your friends and family.

## Put yourself out there

So, you know who you want to help and how and you know that there is a market for your business. The next thing to do is start telling people! You need to put yourself out there, on social media, at networking events, talking to random strangers at the coffee shop.

Start to position yourself as the "go-to" expert in your area of business. Share so much value and information and, at this point, ask for nothing back. Give, give and then give some more.

Don't worry too much at this point about having fancy website, your logo perfect or a professional photoshoot. You'll need something fairly basic to direct people back to, that explains clearly what you do and how to get in touch with you. Perhaps somewhere to house your blog if you intend of having one - which I highly recommend you do.

The goal in the early stages is to create relationships with your ideal clients, share what you do and offer people value so they know where to come when they need you. It's a great opportunity to test which platforms and channels work best for your business and your audience.

But here's the thing. Don't get disheartened. Not every business is a success right off the bat. Not everybody gets clients running up to them as soon as they open their doors. But you can't use this as a reason to give up. You already know that there is a need and a market for what you're offering; now you have to show people just how necessary you are to them. This will take time, consistency and patience. You can't be jumping from one strategy to the next and wondering why nothing is working. Stick it out, give yourself a cut off point and work tirelessly to make it work.

Give away your course, product or service for free to a few friends and acquaintances, track their experiences and share it with your audience. Ask them to provide recommendations and testimonials and refer you to their friends. Word of mouth in the early days, and always, is one of the strongest marketing tools.

This is also where you will need to get used to not just selling your business, but selling YOU. You are the part of your business that makes it unique and your story is an essential part of your brand. This is why I encourage a blog; it's an opportunity to share who you are, why you started your business and why it is so important to you to reach the lives of others (remember, this isn't about the money, it's about changing lives for the better!).

Your audience needs to get to you know, if they know you, they like you and they trust you, they are more likely to buy from you. A great way to earn peoples' trust is to be open, honest and vulnerable. Not all the time. People don't want to learn about your school days if it has no relevance to your business now. I'm saying that you need to be able to let people in, to give them an understanding of who you are, in order for them to warm up to you. For your local audience, this will be a lot easier. You can foster and nurture relationships in person and get to know people in an in-person setting. Online is where you need to get creative, to stand out and have your voice heard. So communicate A LOT! Engage in discussions on Facebook and LinkedIn, add value, give an insight into your life in your Instagram stories, go live on platforms and allow people to ask you questions about what you do - give value, always give value.

Note that these suggestions are not exhaustive, it's a starting point for you - the goal of this book is to inspire you to get started - there's much more work to get done after that!

For now, just get started, much of this will change and work out over time, the best thing you can do is to put yourself out there. Because here's another secret: nobody, not even the most successful_business owners, has it all figured out - so don't wait until you do, just go for it!

# Chapter 9 - Be Extraordinary

Well, there you have it; evidence and examples from fellow military spouses that it is possible to create your own successful business in this crazy lifestyle - and not one that you struggle with, but one that thrives, one that makes a difference in your community and gives you a real sense of purpose.

So, now what?

You've read the case studies, maybe you're feeling inspired or maybe you still think it's not for you, it's too hard, or you don't have the time. Or maybe you'll start next year...

But I want you to stop thinking about these things the way you used to. Re-frame your old excuses and start changing the could- and should-haves, to the will-dos. Start picturing the future you want, the goals you want to achieve and implement your plan to get there.

What will you do to get closer to your goal?

What will you do to find out what your true purpose is?

What legacy will you leave?

You see, we can all "be". It's so easy to go through life as a recipient of whatever is happening to us at the time, heck we can even find joy and happiness doing it, but is that enough for you?

Are you happy to settle for whatever comes your way, or do you want to seize every opportunity like it's your last one and maximise the hell out of it?!

No matter how many opportunities you think we get to live, we only get THIS life, this version of it, one time. No do-overs.

Imagine this is the second chance you've had at your life, your previous "self" is watching everything you're doing now, having already had their chance.

What do you think they'd be saying? Would they be slapping their forehead screaming "WHHYYYYYY are you doing that?" or even "Why AREN'T you doing that?!" Or would they be on the edge of their seat, popcorn flying all over the place because they are so pumped about what you're doing, wishing they'd done it first but rooting you on and on to the next incredible opportunity?!

Sometimes, we need to take a step away from our normal selves, our usual routine and ask if it's what we really DESIRE. Or if it's what's easy, accessible and gets you through. We may even think we're happy. But is it real happiness, or because we haven't experienced what more there is?

I believe that we are all capable of creating change, starting a movement and leaving an unforgettable legacy. I also believe that the vast majority of us will never tap into that side of us, to see what we're capable of – because it can be scary! It takes a lot of self-reflection and self-development and then when we decide to go after it, the fear kicks in.

There's a lot of sacrifice required, a lot of set-backs and reasons why it was a bad idea – it takes strength and a whole lot more to stick your middle finger up at all that and push on through.

If you're sitting there thinking you're not strong enough, I call bullsh*t! You are! You just don't want to admit that you are because that means you have to go and do something about it, and that means risking failure.

WHO CARES?! You know what failing is? An opportunity to learn and do it better the next time, and the next and the next, until you stop failing! Stop thinking of all the reasons and excuses as to why you're not chasing your goals, get out there and start. And fail. Pick yourself up and start again.

I want to leave you with this, my friend:

Be stronger. Be better.

# BE EXTRAORDINARY.

Notes:

**If you'd like to discuss this book further, or how I may be able to help you, you can find me here:**

Email: gems@gemscollins.com

Website: www.gemscollins.com

Facebook: www.facebook.com/ gemscollins1

LinkedIn: www.linkedin.com/in/ gemscollins

Instagram: www.instagram.com/ gems.collins

**Find more information about Airman to Mom here:**

Website: http://www.airmantomom.com

Facebook: http://www.facebook.com/airmantomom

Twitter: http://www.twitter.com/airmantomom

LinkedIn: https://www.linkedin.com/in/airmantomom/

**Find more information about The Seasoned Spouse here:**

Website: www.seasonedspouse.com

Facebook: www.facebook.com/seasonedspouseblog

Instagram: www.instagram.com/theseasonsedspouse

Twitter: www.twitter.com/seasonedspouse


**Find more information about Real Talk with the Ms's here:**

Facebook: www.facebook.com/
tara.tiffany.353

Instagram: www.instagram.com/
realtalkwiththe_ms_s

You can also subscribe to their podcast on iTunes or your favourite podcast platform!


**Find more information about Tiny Troops Soccer® here:**

Facebook: www.facebook.com/
tinytroopssoccer

Website: www.tinytroopssoccer.com

Instagram: www.instagram.com/
tiny_troops_soccer

LinkedIn: http://www.linkedin.com/in/
amytinytroopssoccer

**Find more information about Create
Captivate here:**

Facebook: https://
www.facebook.com/createcaptivate

Instagram: https://
www.instagram.com/createcaptivate/

LinkedIn: https://www.linkedin.com/
company/happy-kaycee-productions